New England's Little Known WAR WONDERS

This book is dedicated to Daniel Howard Cahill, my eldest son, who I hope never sees war. He is one of the most dedicated Americans I know, and if ever called to defend democracy I'm sure will be among the first to respond.

Otis Merrithew of Brookline, Massachusetts, alias William Cutting, America's greatest hero of World War I, at the grave of his patriot ancestor, James Otis, in Boston.   *Photo by George Dow.*

Cover: Engraving of British Retreat from Concord, by James Smillie, couresty Massachusetts Bicentennial Commission.

        ISBN-0-916787-06-0

I
THE RIVER THAT CHANGED AMERICA'S COURSE

Reverend Thomas Barnard was halfway through his lengthy Sunday sermon when the front door of the Old North Church crashed open. All turned in their pews to see a stocky minuteman standing in the doorway. "The British are coming!" he shouted, and the congregation rushed from the church to take up arms at the North Bridge.

The minuteman was not Paul Revere; nor was the place Lexington or Concord — that battle would take place some two months later. The date was February 26, 1775, and the place was Salem, Massachusetts. Here, the British and American forces met for the first time, and American blood was shed on the banks of the North River. This river that plunged America into a war with the world's greatest empire had once before changed the course of American history.

Only six years after the ship MAYFLOWER landed at Plymouth, Roger Conant and a group of friends settled at Naumkeag, now Salem. They chose Naumkeag because of its fine harbor and its two river outlets; one called the South River, the other, the North. A London attorney, John Winthrop, was elected Governor of the colony by the Massachusetts Bay Company, and he arrived in Salem aboard the ship ARBELLA on June 12, 1630. Another ship, the TALBOT, with Governor Winthrop's son Henry aboard, arrived at Salem, 19 days later. On the following day, July 2nd, young Henry decided to visit the Indian settlement in the North Fields on the opposite bank of the narrow river. At the very site where the North Bridge would be built almost 100 years later, Henry attempted to canoe across to the Indian encampment. The river, as usual, was calm, but for some unknown reason the canoe capsized and Henry drowned. The new Governor was so grief stricken at the death of his son that he immediately moved out of Salem to begin a settlement at Charlestown, some 15 miles away. Within a short time, Governor Winthrop and his followers crossed the Mystic River from Charlestown to what is now Boston. Thus, if it were not for the drowning of Henry Winthrop in the North River, Salem and not Boston would now be the capital of Massachusetts, and acclaimed "hub" of America.

Salem did become an unofficial capital of Massachusetts prior to the American Revolution when British General Thomas Gage refused to allow the Massachusetts General Court to sit in Boston. Openly defying Gage's orders, the General Court, made up of such prominent members as John Hancock and Sam Adams, met in Salem and set up a Provincial Congress. From that day on, Gage kept a suspicious eye on the Witch City.

The Provincial Congress made Salem, along with Lexington and Concord, an ordinance depot for weapons that might be needed later. In the same North Fields where the Indians once lived, Captain Richard Derby, famous sailing master, had stashed away 19 cannons and munitions. Although war with Britain was not inevitable, relations were deeply strained. The Colonists believed that they should hide what few heavy weapons they had, before the British confiscated them, for King George, besides establishing an army of regulars in Massachusetts, had also forbidden the Colonists to arm themselves.

Confiscating the arms at Salem was just what General Gage had in mind. A British spy had heard about the cannons in the North Fields and passed the information to Gage. He, in turn, ordered Lieutenant Colonel Alexander Leslie, the son of a Scottish earl, to take a regiment of 250 infantry troops to Salem to seize the hidden arms.

Leslie hid his Redcoats below decks on a British transport that departed Castle William in Boston at midnight on Saturday, February 25, 1775. At 11:00 a.m. on Sunday, the ship dropped anchor off Marblehead, some five miles from the center of Salem, but the troops remained below decks until 2:00 p.m., when Leslie knew the Colonists would be at church services.

Major John Pedrick, Marblehead's Paul Revere, was not fooled, and after watching the troops land at Homan's Cove, he alerted the townspeople of Marblehead and then headed his steed for the road to Salem. Pedrick was a friend of Colonel Leslie   and as he galloped past the colonel and his troops marching to Salem, he cheerfully greeted the colonel and rode on to the center of Salem to spread the alarm.

Church bells began to chime and drums began to roll — the signal that trouble was brewing in Salem Center. Minutemen from every corner of the town grabbed their muskets and headed for the North River, which winds through the center of Salem. Even minutemen from the surrounding villages of Beverly and Danvers came running. When Leslie arrived with his scarlet clad, well disciplined regiment, hundreds of Colonists were at the river to meet him and badgered him and his men with "cat calls" and insults.

"Go home and tell your king he has sent you on a fool's errand," shouted someone from the crowd. "You coward," cried Sarah Tarrant from the open window of her home overlooking the river, "do you think we were born in the woods to be frightened by owls?"

"Shoot me if you have the courage," shouted Bob Foster the blacksmith, "but I doubt it."

Colonel Leslie was so unnerved by the teasing, that when he reached the river, he marched his troops onto the North Bridge and almost into the water before he noticed that the northern leaf of the drawbridge was up, barring further progress.

"Lower the leaf of that bridge at once," he shouted to the armed minutemen on the north bank. No one replied. "Damn you," shouted Leslie, his face flushing to match his uniform, "you are obstructing the King's highway. Lower that bridge I say!"

Colonial farmer James Barr who was standing near Leslie said, matter-of-factly, "you'd best be advised, colonel sir, that this here is a private way. The bridge belongs to the proprietors of the North Field."

"I will go over that bridge if I must wait a month," replied Leslie.

"You may stay as long as you please, no one will care," said Captain John Felt of the Salem Minutemen, who had been keeping to Leslie's side like a shadow.

"If the draw is not closed at once, my men will fire," Leslie shouted at Felt.

"Fire and be damned," replied Felt. "If you fire, you will be a dead man." Felt then raised his hands to Leslie's shoulders and threatened to throw him in the river. It was a cold day and icebergs drifted along the shore. Felt could have easily pushed him off the bridge and Leslie knew it.

Colonel David Mason who was with the minutemen on the north side of the river shouted at Leslie: "You had better look out for the safety of your men, for the entire countryside has been alerted."

"I have come for the cannons," Leslie shouted back, "and I mean to have them."

"They'll never be surrendered," replied Richard Derby who was with Mason on the opposite river bank.

"Turn this company about," Leslie ordered his captain, "and have the men fire." As the Redcoats were about to carry out this order, and the minutemen pulled back the hammers of their flintlocks, Leslie spied a few small boats sitting beside a wharf on the south side of the river near the bridge. Seeing a way to cross the river, he countermanded his order to fire and ordered his troops to board the boats. Felt then shouted to some of his men on the riverbank to scuttle the boats.

Felt's men, Joseph Sprague and Joseph Whicher, got to the boats before the Redcoats did and smashed the bottom out of each one with boulders and axes. The crowd cheered as the Redcoats came at Sprague and Whicher with fixed bayonets.

"Am I forbidden to put holes in my own boat?" laughed Sprague as the British soldiers approached. Joseph Whicher, a black man who worked in Sprague's distillery, leaped to the bow of one of the sinking boats, tore open his shirt and defied a British soldier to kill him. The Redcoat stabbed Whicher in the chest, and he fell back into the boat. Although the wound was not serious, Joseph Whicher of the Witch City became the first casualty in the War for Independence.

Reverend Thomas Barnard, whose sermon was interuppted earlier in the day, recognized the impasse for what it was — both sides were forming and a Revolution was about to begin. He suggested a compromise. Since Leslie was under orders to search the environs of the North Bridge and to seize any weapons found there, Barnard suggested to Captain Felt that Leslie be allowed to cross the bridge, but to travel no further. Felt and Barnard realized that some of the cannons that had been hidden under the bridge earlier that day had been moved deep into the North Fields. Felt reluctantly agreed, as did Leslie. Leslie was usually a quiet, easygoing man who certainly did not want to begin a war with America unless he was forced to.

The draw was lowered and Colonel Leslie with his troops was allowed to cross the bridge, but then he ordered them to turn right around and march back over the bridge — and they returned to Marblehead and their ship. The Colonials cheered and jeered as the British marched away, and the incident is known to this day as "Leslie's Retreat."

Major Pedrick rode back to Marblehead ahead of the troops and set out some wine at his home for Colonel Leslie and his officers, but Leslie never showed up. The furious General Gage, calling Leslie names similar to those used by Sarah Tarrant, had the colonel court-martialed and shipped back to Scotland.

In London, Gentlemen's Magazine's lead story was about Leslie's Retreat. "The Americans have hoisted their standard of liberty at Salem," reported the magazine to the British people, "and there is no doubt that the next news will be an account of a bloody battle engagement between the two armies..." The next account received was after the battle of Lexington and Concord, and it was Richard Derby, whose cannons Leslie was after in Salem, who sailed to England and arrived before General Gage's messenger to bring the British first news of open warfare.

It was soon after the Salem incident that Lord Dartmouth sent General Gage a letter stating that the British Parliament and king considered Massachusetts in a state of rebellion, and they gave Gage the authority "to impose martial law — a test should be made to see if these Colonials are willing to fight...If there is to be war, let it be brought about immediately, before they (the Colonials) can develop an army..."

It is obvious that General Gage gave explicit orders to Lieutenant Colonel Smith and Major Pitcairn not to repeat Leslie's cowardice act at Lexington and Concord, which should leave no doubt in any historian's mind as to who fired the first shot heard 'round the world.

Some five months after the Battle of Lexington and Concord, at the mouth of the North River, where it meets the Danvers River and flows into Beverly Harbor separating Salem and Beverly, the first ship of the American Navy was commissioned by General George Washington. The schooner HANNAH, owned by General John Glover and manned by Marbleheaders, sailed out to sea from what is now the base of the Salem-Beverly Bridge, to take on the world's greatest Navy. Out to sea only a few days, she was chased back into Beverly Harbor on October 10th, 1775 by the British warship HMS NAUTILUS. The HANNAH accidentally grounded on a sand bar near shore and the NAUTILUS began bombarding her. Soon, cannons from Fort Lee, on the Salem side of the harbor, began bombarding the NAUTILUS. She immediately returned cannon fire but then also became grounded on a sand bar. This battle between the NAUTILUS, the HANNAH and Fort Lee lasted for three hours. It is considered by many American historians to be America's first Naval sea battle, which is somewhat ironic, since neither vessel was afloat at the time.

When the tide came in, the NAUTILUS, with tattered sails and a battered hull, managed to escape back out to sea. No British man-of-war dared enter Salem or Beverly Harbors again during the Revolutionary War. During the battle, only one British sailor was killed and another lost his leg. One American, David Newall of Salem, was wounded when his hand was blown off while loading a cannon.

There is no plaque or monument to this first Naval battle, and only a small plaque, hardly noticable to passers-by, on the North Street overpass, to commemorate Leslie's Retreat. It reads:

"In the Revolution the first Armed Resistance to the Royal Authority was made at the Bridge (26 Feb. 1775) by the people of Salem. The advance of 300 British Troops led by Lt. Col. Leslie and sent by Gen. Gage to seize Munitions of War, was here arrested."

There is a small restaurant-pub on the north side of the North Street overpass, called "Leslie's Retreat", which contains photos, sketches, and documents concerning America's first armed resistance to the throne. In keeping with the Colonial spirit, among other mouth watering delights available at Leslie's, is its famous "British Fort"— all the pancakes you can eat for $1.00. But only a stone's throw away, the North River, the river that in many ways changed the course of American history, still meanders its way into Beverly Harbor. it is steeped with debris, cluttered, dirty and polluted, a terrible tribute to a river that should be a national landmark.

Painting of Leslie's Retreat, 1775, and photo of celebration at North Bridge, Salem in 1875, courtesy Essex Institute and Leslie's Retreat Restaurant, Salem, MA.

II
THE DAY UNCLE SAM WAS BORN

The Wilson children were awakened by the sound of hoofbeats on the Medford Road and the constant shouting of the horseman, "the British are coming!". It was the night of April 18, 1775 and Paul Revere was alerting the village of Menotomy, now Arlington, Massachusetts. The villagers were soon up in arms: the men mustering at Cooper's Tavern at the corner of the Medford and Concord Roads, and the women and children trekking through the back woods to homes that would be far away from the fighting. Mrs. Wilson and her flock of 13 children headed for the Prentiss farm away from the village, but her sons Joe, age 15, Eben, age 13, and Sam, age 8½, begged her to let them stay with their dad and join the fight - she, of course, refused.

By noon, word arrived in Menotomy of the battles of Lexington and Concord, and Minutemen from other villages and towns arrived to join the Menotomy men, setting up skirmish lines along the Concord Road to welcome the British as they marched back to Boston.

Seven Danvers Minutemen hid behind the stone wall beside the meetinghouse, across the Concord Road from Cooper's Tavern. Other North Shore men from Peabody, Beverly, Lynn and Salem took cover some 800 feet up the road near the house and barn of Jason Russell, with five Minutemen from Needham and Dedham. "Old Man" Russell, as he was called, only 59 years old, but lame, had set up his own little barricade in his front yard facing Concord Road. He, like Mrs. Wilson, had escorted his wife and son to the Prentiss farm, but returned home to join in the fray. His neighbors, Mr. Wilson, Jabez Wyman, Jason Winship and Ammi Cutter, tried to persuade him to join them across the road behind Mill Brook, where they could snipe at the British, but the Redcoats couldn't get at them unless they forded the brook. Russell refused to move, saying, "my home is my castle and I shall defend it."

The British troops, angry and exhausted, entered Menotomy about 4 p.m. Minutemen hiding behind trees and stone walls had been shooting at them all the way from Concord, and many had fallen dead or wounded by the wayside. The bloodiest fighting, however, was at Menotomy, for British reinforcements from Boston entered the village about the same time retreating Redcoats were coming up the Concord Road.

The Wilson Boys were now chomping at the bit — they could hear the distant drum rolls, the repeating blasts of musket fire, and there was a smell of burnt powder in the cool spring air. Even young Sam Wilson knew that something exciting and important was happening — America was being born, and it was fitting as it was ironic that he should be there, for he was to become the very symbol of this new nation — Uncle Sam.

Sam's father, with Wyman and Winship, fired at the oncoming Redcoats, then retreated into the woods. Ammi Cutter tried to cross the road again to warn Jason Russell of the hundreds of British reinforcements that he could see assembling on the high ridge behind Jason's house, but Redcoats coming up the road shot at him and he fell. The British thought they had killed Cutter, but he was only scratched. He waited until they passed, then got up and ran for his house. Wyman and Winship decided to stop for a drink at Cooper's Tavern, as Wilson continued on to the South. It was their last drink, for the Redcoats barged into the tavern and killed them.

Across the road, the Danvers and Peabody Minutemen were forced to retreat, joining the other 19 Minutemen behind Jason Russell's barricade. They had stopped the British column coming up the road, but when the reinforcements attacked them from the ridge behind the house they were completely surrrounded and greatly outnumbered. The Minutemen raced for the house. The Danvers and Peabody men,who waited to be last in the front door, didn't make it — their bullet-ridden bodies covered the front lawn. Jason Russell didn't make it into the house either — he was caught by two musket balls in the head, right at his front door where he slumped dead on the stoop.

In the kitchen, Dan Townsend and Timothy Munro, from Lynn, struggled to hold the back door as Redcoats tried to break it in. Losing the struggle, Townsend made a desperate leap through the kitchen window to escape, but broken glass slashed his throat before he hit the ground. As Redcoats crashed into the kitchen, Munro followed Townsend through the window and remarkably landed on his feet. Four Redcoats greeted him in the backyard, but he dodged their bayonets and raced for the Watertown Road, a platoon of Regulars hard on his heels. Musketballs slashed his skin, but he kept on running as fast as he could with, seemingly, the entire British Army after him. Panting like a dog and bloody from head to toe, he made it to the Prentiss farm. Timothy was the first casualty that the women and children hiding there had seen, and he had bad news for Mrs. Russell and her son Noah. This bloody sight of a Minuteman,who escaped death by the skin of his teeth, was an image that Uncle Sam would remember to his dying day.

As Munro made good his escape, a furious hand-to-hand battle ensued inside the Russell home, in every room. A British soldier who was there later reported what happened: "The house was long defended by eight resolute fellows, but the grenadiers at last got possession when, after having run their bayonets into seven, the eighth continued to abuse them with all the beastlike rage of a true Cromwellian, and but a moment before he quitted this world, applied such epithets as I must leave unmentioned."

After the slaughter, the dead Minutemen were dragged into the kitchen by the Redcoats and piled into a bloody heap, to be left there for Mrs. Russell to find when she returned home. "The blood in that room was almost ankle deep," she later reported. Three Redcoats were killed inside the house. Among the dead Minutemen in the kitchen were: Benjamin Pierce of Salem, William Flint, Thomas Hadley and Abe Ramsdell of Lynn; and Reuben Kennison of Beverly.

Most Beverly Minutemen, however, remained unscathed. Eight of them cleverly found refuge in the fruit cellar under the house and remained there during the battle with their muskets pointing up the stairs to the only entryway. The one British soldier who tried to follow them was shot dead immediately upon opening the fruit cellar door. They and Timmy Munro were the only survivors in the fiercest fight of the day.

Before the Revolutionary War was over, the Wilsons sold their home in Menotomy to Thomas Russell and moved to Mason, New Hampshire, just over the Massachusetts line, where four of Jason Russell's family had moved before the battle. Sam Wilson spent the remainder of his youth in Mason, and at age 22, struck out for upstate New York with his brother Eben. They settled at Troy and together started a meat-packing business. The business flourished so they set up their younger brother Nat Wilson in another meat-packing company at Catskill, New York. In 1797, Sam returned to Mason, New Hampshire to marry his childhood sweetheart, Betsey Mann. At the wedding was Betsey's first cousin from Springfield, Massachusetts, John Chapman, who had also been a childhood friend of Sam's. Like Sam, he too would become an important hero in American folklore, known throughout the nation as Johnny Appleseed.

Sam and Betsey returned to Troy, 150 miles by sleigh, and it was there Betsey met for the first time, the packing plant foreman, Jonas W. Gleason. Gleason, a large jocular man from County Cork, Ireland, and possibly an ancestor of comedian Jackie Gleason, was Sam Wilson's best friend. Sam and Jonas "would go considerable lengths to make a good joke," writes Sam's biographer, Lucius Wilson. They often played tricks on each other, to the amusement of the 200 meat-packing employees. On March 17th of each year, Jonas would see to it that something in the meat-packing plant or yard was painted a bright green to surprise Sam. One year it was his desk, another year he painted one of the bulls in the yard, and on March 17, 1811, Sam's children showed up at the plant with green hair, thanks to Gleason. On the Fourth of July, which was also the seasonal closing of the meat-packing trade, Gleason would lead a large parade on horseback to Uncle Sam's picnic and "blow-out". One year Gleason dressed as a bull, with horns, tail, "and wearing a huge pair of bullock livers as epaulets, " Lucius Wilson reports. In another parade, Gleason rode a bull to the picnic, to the delight of the local children. Sam and Betsey were so good to the children of Troy that they were known as Uncle Sam and Aunt Betsey. Gleason picked up the nicknames from the children and from then on always referred to his friend and boss as "Uncle Sam". "It was Gleason the Irishman," Lucius Wilson tells us, "who made the observation that launched the Uncle Sam legend."

During the War of 1812, the Wilson Meat-Packing Company sold large consignments of beef to the Army. On a routine inspection of the plant and yard by dignitaries, including the Governor of New York, they noticed that all the barrels had "U.S." stamped on them. Sam had stamped them to signify United States property, but Jonas Gleason told the visiting dignitaries that the initials stood for "Uncle Sam". Everyone had a good laugh over the comment, but no one at the time realized that Gleason's joke had launched Uncle Sam as the patron saint of America. Within a few weeks there were broadsides posted about New York with a caricature of Sam Wilson as "Uncle Sam". Before the war was over, American soldiers were being called "Uncle Sam's boys," and soon, all items belonging to the government were marked "U.S.". After the war, Sam Wilson was constantly called on to be a toastmaster or to give political speeches. In 1837, he became Chairman of the Democratic Committee. Sam Wilson died at age 87 in 1854 and newspapers mourned the passing of "Uncle Sam", but Sam wasn't dead — he was revived in 1916, when prominent illustrator James Montgomery Flagg painted Sam's portrait, and the War Department added the words: "I Want You" to the painting, using it as a World War I recruiting poster.

Hardly a week goes by these days that you don't see a cartoon, illustration, or reference to "Uncle Sam", and all due to the prank of Jonas Gleason. The real Sam, however, to his dying day, never could forget the tattered, scarred and blood-soaked Minuteman who escaped the wrath of the British at Jason Russell's house. To Sam Wilson, Timothy Munro of Lynn, Massachusetts was the real Uncle Sam.

Timothy Munro died at age 72, on March 1, 1808 - until his dying day he kept the clothes he wore on April 19, 1775: a waistcoat with all the buttons shot off it and an overcoat with 32 bullet holes in it. He often recalled that as he ran through the British lines from Russell's house that day, a British soldier shouted, "That damned Yankee is indestructible" - and so is what Tim Munro stood for.

Jason Russell house in Arlington, MA. where bloodiest battle took place on April 19, 1775. Minuteman stands inside door of Russell House. Outside the door, Russell himself was killed by Redcoats, as were seven other Massachusetts Minutemen, plus nine inside the house.

Uncle Sam's house in Mason, New Hampshire. Photo T. Smith. The frigate CHESAPEAKE, defeated by the British off Swampscott, MA, but her Commander's cry, "Don't give up the ship!" rallied America to victory in the War of 1812.

III
CURSE OF THE "CHESAPEAKE"

Hundreds of spectators were usually present at the launching of a new American warship. Viewers would cheer and applaud as the ship splashed into the water, unfurled her sails and headed for sea with an excited and eager crew aboard. Such was not the case with the 36-gun frigate CHESAPEAKE. There were no crowds to cheer her at the christening, only silent stern-faced yard workers who gave her fleeting glances. The crowd had been there the day before, but were disappointed when the massive sailing ship was wedged in her cradle halfway down the ways and wouldn't budge. The superstitous shipyard workers considered this a bad omen. When she finally splashed in next day, and her sails were set, the crew found her difficult to manuever. On her way out of the harbor, she stuck fast on a sandbar. "Another indication." the workers mumbled amongst themselves, "that the CHESAPEAKE was cursed." Even after she was able to slip off the sandbar and managed to sail to the mouth of the Chesapeake Bay, she moved erratically and reacted slowly to her skipper's commands. Her 300-man crew also believed the ship could be in jeopardy at sea because of her sluggishness.

Under the command of Commodore James Barron, the CHESA-PEAKE finally anchored in the bay, ready for her first assignment to sail to the Mediterranean Sea to relieve the frigate CONSTITUTION that patrolled those pirate infested waters. Also anchored at the mouth of Chesapeake Bay were six British men-o-war. The year was 1807, and although Britain and America were not yet at war, relations between these two countries were strained, mainly because of England's desire to impress American seamen into the King's service against their will. American captains were not as notorious for impressing British tars, but the food was better and the discipline less harsh aboard U.S. ships. Therefore, many tars, when they had the chance, jumped ship to join the Americans.

Unbeknownst to Commodore Barron, four British seamen, deserters from the HMS MELAMPUS anchored nearby, had signed on as crew members aboard the CHESAPEAKE. Before the CHESA-PEAKE sailed, the MELAMPUS commander learned that four tars were aboard the American ship. He demanded their return through the Secretary of the American Navy, Robert Smith. Smith in turn wrote to Barron: "You will be pleased to make full inquiry relative to these men," he ordered, "and you will immediately direct the recruiting officer in no case to enter deserters from British ships of war."

Commodore Barron held his inquiry and replied to Smith that all the so-called British deserters were in fact Americans, who had earlier been impressed by the British: "William Ware was pressed by the MELAMPUS from an American schooner in the Bay of Biscay in 1805; Daniel Martin was impressed at the same time and is a native of Westport, Massachusetts; John Strachan and John Little are also Americans . . ."

With the four ex-MELAMPUS crewmen aboard, the CHESAPEAKE sailed for the Mediterranean on June 22, 1807. Setting sail from Chesapeake Bay that same day was the 50-gun British frigate LEOPARD.

Within a few hours, the LEOPARD was sailing beside the smaller CHESAPEAKE. The sea was calm and the crews of both ships were tense as sails were lowered. A longboat carrying a British lieutenant and eight tars rowed to the CHESAPEAKE's gangway. Commodore Barron greeted them:

"Commodore Douglass of the LEOPARD is fully determined to recover deserters that are now harbored on board this ship," snapped the terse British lieutenant. "It is my desire to warn you that it is best that you submit to a peaceable search."

"I cannot permit a search of my vessel," was Barron's reply.

The British lieutenant's face flushed, and he ordered his tars to row back to the LEOPARD. The officers aboard the CHESAPEAKE asked Barron to clear the decks for action. They did not trust the British, but Barron did not think it necessary. "I'm sure that this is the end of the entire incident," he commented.

The CHESAPEAKE's guns were not primed, the powder horns were locked in the magazine room, and matches were not available on deck to light the gun fuses. When the roar of cannons erupted from the decks of the LEOPARD, the CHESAPEAKE was unprepared to defend herself. Wood splinters, blocks and spars flew across the deck as a broadside struck the CHESAPEAKE. Her decks were soon splattered with blood.

"Priming horns, give us priming horns and matches," cried young lieutenant Henry Allen to the stunned Commodore Barron. Seeing that Barron was frozen with fear and outrage, Lieutenant Allen ran to the main hatch and scrambled below decks to grab a red hot coal from the galley stove. Juggling the coal in his hands, he quickly returned to the deck and handed it to a gunner who had primed his cannon. As the gunner dropped the coal in the breech, a ball from the LEOPARD struck him dead. Lieutenant Allen managed to fire the cannon and, although the ball did no damage to the British ship, it was the only reply from the CHESAPEAKE to twenty minutes of constant bombardment from the LEOPARD.

"Haul down our flag," commanded Barron.

"Please, sir, give us a chance to fight like men," cried Lieutenant Allen.

Barron gave the command again and a crewman lowered the American flag. The LEOPARD ceased her firing.

"Sir, you have disgraced us," said Allen to Barron, his hands burned raw from the hot coal. Barron turned from the young lieutenant and wept.

The British boarded the CHESAPEAKE stepping over many wounded and moaning American crewmen on deck. They searched the ship and took away William Ware, Daniel Martin, John Strachen and John Little in irons.

The CHESAPEAKE limped back to America where Commodore James Barron was relieved of his command and sentenced to five years retirement from the Navy without pay. Now, in addition to being considered a "cursed ship", America's newest frigate was openly called, "The Cowardly CHESAPEAKE."

Many Americans believed at the time, that the CHESAPEAKE incident was the spark that led America into the war with Britain in 1812. For six, long uneventful years, the CHESAPEAKE sailed from port to port, her unflattering nicknames following her into every seaside pub and cafe, causing many a barroom brawl and an occasional duel on a lonely beach.

The War of 1812 brought many a credo for her sister ship, the battling frigate CONSTITUTION, dubbed "Old Ironsides," but not one encouraging word for the CHESAPEAKE.

Ironically, the CHESAPEAKE was anchored in the CONSTITUTION's home port of Charlestown, Massachusetts when the opportunity came to vindicate herself. Her commander, in May of 1813, was 32 year old Captain James Lawrence. Lawrence had made it known to his superior, Captain William Bainbridge, who was in charge of the Charlestown Navy Yard that he would much prefer being skipper of "Old Ironsides."

"If I had the CONSTITUTION, " Lawrence told Bainbridge, "this English captain would not be flaunting his flag at the harbor mouth."

The 52-gun British ship SHANNON had for four days stood in close to Boston Light House at the mouth of Boston Harbor. She was in sight of the CHESAPEAKE at anchor in the inner harbor, and British Captain Brake was taunting the notorious American frigate to come out and do battle.

"Give me the chance to wipe the stain from the CHESAPEAKE's name," Captain Lawrence begged Bainbridge at the officer's club on the night of May 31.

"Your ship is in no condition to fight at the moment," replied Bainbridge. "She has a green crew and her new running gear has not been properly tested."

Over 100 of Lawrence's crew had never been to sea and his first lieutenant was only 21 years old, and had never seen action.

"I will go to the yard and get workers who are not employed to join my crew," insisted Lawrence. "I must fight this fellow."

Bainbridge begrudgingly agreed but, by next morning, Lawrence was able to recruit only 60 yard workers. Few desired to board the cursed ship, let alone fight on her, no matter how high the pay.

Before noon, Lawrence was aboard the CHESAPEAKE with his few motley recruits. He quickly mustered them with his green crew and inexperienced officers, two of whom were only midshipmen acting as lieutenants. "Men of the CHESAPEAKE," shouted the weary Commander, who had been up all night searching for men to supplement his crew, "it is our good fortune to be able to answer the call that our country has made upon our honor. We will answer it with our lives, if necessary. Do your duty, fight well and nobly . . . To your stations!"

The regular navy men moved quickly, but the yard workers stood fast on deck. A bedraggled spokesman stepped forward and demanded pay "now", before the fighting began. Lawrence's face reddened. He considered their demands outrageous, even treasonous, but he feared a mutiny, and he needed every hand to face the SHANNON.

"Take these men to the cabin and pay them," he shouted to his first lieutenant, "and a double allowance of grog for all."

It was noon on a beautiful cloudless day as the CHESAPEAKE weighed anchor. Word of the upcoming battle spread through Charlestown, Boston and the North Shore from Salem to Winthrop. Thousands of spectators lined the shores or set out in small boats to watch what they considered might be the greatest sea fight of the war.

Flaunting the union jack, the SHANNON, under the able direction of Captain Brake, began maneuvering into good firing position as the CHESAPEAKE headed towards her. It wasn't until 4:00 p.m., some seven miles off the coast of Swamspcott that the first shot was fired by the CHESAPEAKE. She had sailed into an advantageous position to rack the SHANNON's decks. The discharge from the SHANNON's cannons was almost simultaneous, but much more devastating. Ten American crewmen and two officers died immediately, and 23 were badly wounded, including Captain Lawrence who received a severe wound in the leg. The CHESAPEAKE's bulwarks were crushed and her main cabin was in splinters. The two ships were within pistol shot of each other now and, at this close range, both fired three consecutive broadsides. The CHESAPEAKE's top sail was shot away, but the SHANNON received a gaping hole below the waterline, and she started to sink. Placed in the rigging of the SHANNON, however, were four British marine marksmen, and one found a bead on Lawrence's gold epaulets. He fired, and a musketball tore through Lawrence's chest.

"Don't give up the ship . . . don't give up the ship," Lawrence gasped to young Lieutenant William Cox who knelt before him. Cox, also wounded in the neck and shoulder, was awed and sickened by the sights and sounds of battle around him. He watched as the SHANNON's skipper tried to lock his ship to the CHESAPEAKE's gunwales to keep her afloat, and the CHESAPEAKE, as sluggish and unmaneuverable as ever, could not resist the attempt. Smoke, and the smell of powder filled the air, as men screamed in frustration and anger, and men without limbs cried in pain and terror. Cox tried unsuccessfully to lift Lawrence to his feet, then called for crewmen to carry him below. Lieutenant Ballard had his leg shot off. Mr. White, the master of the ship, was dead and the lieutenant of the American marines was mortally wounded, along with the ship's boatswain.

While Cox was below and the CHESAPEAKE was without a commander, Captain Brake managed to tangle the SHANNON's lower rigging to the CHESAPEAKE's anchor line. The ships were now interlocked, saving the SHANNON from sinking. Captain Brake then led a boarding party onto the CHESAPEAKE's main deck. Swords and cutlasses flashed as the British and Americans wrestled in hand-to-hand combat.

Below deck, under the surgeon's knife, Lawrence pleaded with the tearful Lieutenant Cox to rally the crew. Cox raced on deck and attempted to lead the Americans to victory, but he could see it was of no use, the British were slaughtering his men. The American flag was hauled down, and the British signaled their victory to the thousands of spectators lining the shore.

Captain Brake received a severe sword wound in the head and was unconscious, but 200 British tars, marines, and officers were now aboard the CHESAPEAKE. Captain Lawrence, in a delirium below deck, shouted, "Do not strike the colors. While I live, they shall wave."

Lawrence remained alive for four days without uttering another word. Captain Brake survived his wound, but 26 of his men were killed and 56 were wounded. Of the CHESAPEAKE's crew, 48 were killed and 98 wounded. Although the SHANNON sustained the greatest damage, she was able to escort the CHESAPEAKE into the British Port of Halifax, Nova Scotia, where she was literally ripped apart by souvenir hunting British soldiers and sailors. Captain Lawrence died in Halifax, and was buried by the British Navy on June 4, with complete military honors. A few days later, Captain George Crowninshield of Salem, Massachusetts was sent to Halifax by the American government to exhume Lawrence's body and bring it back to Salem.

Unfortunately, young Lieutenant Cox was made the scapegoat for America's disgrace at losing the CHESAPEAKE. At the court martial, he was charged with cowardice for leaving the main deck at the height of the battle, while he was unknowingly in command of the ship. He was forced to leave the Navy, but, determined to clear his name, Cox enlisted as a private in the American Army. All his life, he and his family attempted to have his name reinstated into Naval ranks, but they were unsuccessful. The curse of the CHESAPEAKE continued to haunt her officers and crew long after she had been unceremoniously stripped to the waterline in Halifax. No less than five duels were fought between her officers and ex-crew men with intimidating sailors and civilians who spoke too loudly about the "cowardly" ship.

The most popular song of the time, heard at British rugby games and in the forecastles of ships of every nation was a fast moving little ditty titled "The Chesapeake." Its verses went as follows:

1. *"Oh the Chesapeake so bold out of Boston we are told,*
   Came to take a British frigate neat and handy-o,
   And the people all in port, they came out to see the sport
   With their music playing Yankee Doodle-Dandy-O.

2. *Ere the action had begun and the Yankees made much fun,*
   Saying: 'We'll tow her up to Boston neat and handy-o,
   And after that we'll dine, treat our sweethearts all with wine,
   And we'll dance a jig of Yankee Doodle Dandy-O.'

3. *The British frigate's name, that for the purpose came*
   To cool the Yankee's courage neat and handy-o,
   Was the Shannon, Captain Brake, whose crew wore hearts of oak,
   And for fightin' were allowed to be grandy-o.

4. *The fight was scarce begun when Yanks flinched from their guns;*
   They thought that they had worked us neat and handy-o.
   Then Brake he drew his sword, crying 'Now my lads we'll board,
   And we'll stop their playing Yankee Doodle Dandy-O, Yankee
   Doodle, Yankee Doodle, Dandy-O.'

5. *When the Britons heard this word, they quickly sprang on board*
   And seized the Yankee ensign neat and handy-o.
   Not withstanding all their brags, now the glorious British flag
   At the Yankee mizzen-peak was quite the dandy-o."

One of the most famous CHESAPEAKE duels was fought seven years after she was captured, and during a time when America was finally enjoying a renewed peace with Britain.

The greatest Naval hero of the War of 1812 was Stephen Decatur. He also had been an outspoken member of the court martial that suspended Commodore Barron from the Navy for five years after the first CHESAPEAKE disgrace. Adding insult to injury, after the court martial, Decatur had been offered command of the CHESAPEAKE. When Barron returned to the Navy after the War of 1812, he demanded the command of another ship, but the reason the Navy never met this demand is that Stephen Decatur was aware that Barron had lived in England during the war, and after the war, he wrote to Barron from Washington saying: "Your conduct has been such as to forever bar your readmission into the service . . ."

Barron replied on January 16, 1820 from Norfolk, Virginia: "Your letter of the 29th I have received. In it you say you have now to inform me that you shall pay no further attention to any communication that I may make to you, other than direct call to the field; in answer to which I have only one reply that wherever you will consent to meet me on fair and equal grounds, that is, such as two honorable men may consider just and proper, you are at liberty to view this as that call. The whole tenor of your conduct to me justifies this course of proceeding on my part . .."

Decatur accepted his challenge and the date was set for March 14 in a field at Bladenburg, Maryland. A Captain Elliot was Barron's second, and Captain Bainbridge, who had tried to stop Lawrence from challenging the SHANNON, was Decatur's second. Bainbridge mentions that on the morning of the duel, "Young Decatur was quite cheerful and did not desire to take Barron's life." The young American hero had faced death many times in battle and had fought and won his share of duels. The four men arrived at the field, which flanked a brook called Blood Run, at dawn. Barron was nearsighted, so it was agreed that the distance would be only eight paces before the two Naval officers would fire their pistols at one another.

"I hope to meet you in another world," said Barron to Decatur as the seconds loaded their dueling pistols, "and I hope that we be better friends there than we have been here."

The signal was given, and both men fired almost simultaneously. Barron fell as Decatur gripped his right side. Decatur soon fell to his knees and asked to be moved beside the limp body of Barron. Decatur asked Barron's forgiveness. "I forgive you from the bottom of my heart," gasped Barron. Both men were bleeding profusely, but insisted they not be moved by their seconds.

"Why did you not return to America upon the outbreak of hostilities with England?" asked Decatur.

"I will tell you what I expected never to tell a living man," said Barron. "I was a debtor in an English prison."

"Oh, Barron, had I known that, the purse of the service would have been at your disposal, and you and I would not have been lying here."

Barron did not hear him. He was dead.

Decatur was moved by carriage to Washington and died later that evening. The greatest hero of the War of 1812, and the disgraced Commander who was most responsible for starting the war, had killed each other, the final victims of the "cursed CHESAPEAKE."

IV
WHEN THE SOUTH ROSE AGAIN IN VERMONT

The war was on in America, but far away to the South, our New England boys seemed to be making good progress against the Confederates. The single New England girls, however, especially those living in rural villages and towns weren't making much progress at all, for most of the eligible males were off fighting. That's why the handsome, well dressed young man who moved into Room 6 of the Tremont Boarding House on Main Street, St. Albans, Vermont, caught the eye and fancy of fellow boarders, Sarah Clark and Margaret Smith. He and his friend, who wasn't bad looking either, arrived in town on the Montreal Express on October tenth, and it looked like they were going to stay awhile. Both girls liked the taller quiet one with the sleepy hazel eyes and the wavy brown hair. He said hello to them each morning at breakfast or when he squeezed past them in the narrow corridor. He was well-mannered, polite and clean shaven, whereas the other, who looked a bit older, seemed gruff and preoccupied. One early evening, Sarah heard the younger man reading aloud in his room. He was reading Bible scripture, which made her even more interested. She inquired through the house-clerk and found that his name was Bennett H. Young from St. Johns, Canada, a divinity student, and his friend was William Hutchinson, also of St. Johns. "Just came down to Vermont for a holiday, or maybe to buy horses, cause they've been asking about the stables in town," the clerk told Sarah.

On the third morning since their arrival, Bennett Young struck up a conversation with the girls at breakfast. Then, he asked Sarah to have dinner with him on the next evening at the American Hotel, St. Alban's finest. Sarah was thrilled. At dinner they talked about the quaintness of St. Albans and about Biblical prophecies. On a stroll down Main Street after dinner, Sarah pointed out all the places of interest, including Taylor Park across from the hotel, and the grand home of Governor Smith off Bank Street. Bennett Young asked if they could visit the Governor's grounds and stables sometime soon. Since Sarah knew the Governor's family well, a date was set for the following Saturday morning. During the tour of the estate, Young seemed especially interested in the fine horses in the stables, as Sarah tried to contain herself from revealing that her only interest was the young Mister Young himself. Her roomate Margaret Smith warned her that she was falling in love too quickly, and that she knew very little about this visiting Canadian — Sarah took the warning as sour-grapes.

The following Tuesday was Market Day in St. Albans, and Main Street was packed with not only the approximate 1,600 residents of the village, but almost double that, with people coming up from Burlington or down from Canada to buy and sell. It was an exciting day, but not for Sarah, for she only once caught a glimpse of Bennett Young in the crowd, going from shop to shop with his friend Hutchinson, and talking for a time with three other men who got off the train carrying large leather satchels strapped to their shoulders.

Next day, Wednesday, October 19, 1864, was dull in more ways than one. The morning started off with a light drizzle and there was hardly anyone on Main Street. Most of the St. Albans men had left for the legislative session in Montpelier or the court opening at Burlington. The market people who hadn't left the night before were off on the morning train or coach. In the afternoon, the sky threatened more rain. Sarah was coming out of Kingman Store, less than a block from the Tremont House, when the town clock struck three bells — that's when she saw the love of her life for the last time. He was wearing a purple shirt, coon-skin hat and a white rain coat. He was riding at full speed down Main Street towards her, with three other riders behind him. In his right hand he held a gun, waving it over his head, and in the other, a fire bomb, which he threw at a store front, where it exploded into flames. "We are Confederate soldiers," he shouted to the three or four people on the street. "There are hundreds of us and we have come to burn down your town." One man on the street started running for shelter into a store. "What's that man running for?" cried Young. "Where the hell is he going? Shoot the damned cuss!" added the divinity student, to Sarah's great horror. Several shots rang out, but the man made it inside the store. Les Cross, another St. Albans man, came out the door of his saloon when he heard the gunshots. "What the hell are you celebrating?" he asked Young. "You'll find out," replied Young and he shot at Cross, missing his head by an inch. Cross rushed back into his saloon. Then Young threw another of his bottle bombs, known as Greek Liquid Fire, at Atwood's Store, where he saw another man duck in the door, but it had little effect. One of the other horsebacked Confederates threw a bottle of the liquid at the American Hotel outhouse, where another pedestrian was cowering, but it didn't ignite. Young and his men raced up and down Main Street, screeching the Rebel yell and firing their large Naval Colt revolvers, but the only initial reaction along the muddy deserted road was the whinnying of a few horses tied to hitching posts outside the stores and shops. Sarah ran sobbing to the Tremont House, disgusted at what she saw and heard. Margaret Smith had been right . . . Never trust a stranger.

Meanwhile, Young's roommate, William Hutchinson, was next door to the hotel, at the counter of the Franklin County Bank talking to the cashier. The only other person in the bank was an old bearded woodcutter named Jackson Clark, who was sitting by the stove, keeping an ear to the conversation. Four men wearing white overcoats entered and one drew a Naval revolver and pointed it at the cashier. Jackson Clark made a bee-line for the back door, but was wrestled down by one of the white coated intruders. "We are Confederate soldiers," Hutchinson then revealed to Marcus Beardsley, "we have come to rob your bank." Beardsly led them to the vault, and while they filled their leather bags to the brim with greenbacks, Jackson Clark tried to make another break for it, but he was recaptured before he made the door. Hutchinson then decided to lock Clark in the vault and to throw the cashier in with him. "The vault is air-tight," said Beardsly, "no man can live for long in there." "No matter," replied Hutchinson, "we're going to burn down the town, so you'll suffocate either way." He pushed Beardsley in with Clark and locked the vault.

Diagonally across the Main Street from the Franklin County Bank, next to Taylor Park, also known as the Village Green, was the First National Bank of St. Albans. Inside were cashier Albert Sowles and General John Nason, 90 years old and almost totally deaf. First, two men in white overcoats entered the bank and drew revolvers from under their coats. Sowles described the revolvers as being a foot and a half long. "You are my prisoner," said one, "and if you resist, I'll shoot you dead," said the other. Then, two more in white coats entered the bank and went right to the bank safe without saying a word. They took mostly treasury notes and U.S. bonds, stuffing them into their leather bags; bags that they had carried with them on the train from Canada. One of the surley bank robbers was Joseph McGrorty, at age 38, the oldest of the group. Pointing his gun at Sowles, he demanded to know where the gold was. "There is no gold," replied the cashier nervously. "What's in these five bags then?" asked McGrorty, kicking over one of the heavy bags inside the safe. "Just pennies," said Sowles. McGrorty didn't believe him, and he cut the rope sealing the bags. When pennies rolled out, McGrorty was satisfied and he left the safe, as Sowles breathed a sigh of relief— one of the bags contained gold, and it was missed by the robbers. During the robbery, which lasted only twelve minutes, General Nason sat in the middle of the room reading a newspaper. When the Rebels left, he turned to Sowles and asked, "What gentlemen were those?"

Just a few doors up Main Street from the Franklin County Bank, at the corner of Kingman Street, was the Bank of St. Albans. Here, when the town clock struck three, Charles Bishop, cashier, was counting money at the counter and clerk Martin Seymour was in the back room, also counting money. Five men in white overcoats walked in and displayed their Naval revolvers, an apparent favorite weapon with these bold Rebels. The leader of the five, Thomas Collins, was more explicit about their mission than the other two bank robbing chiefs had been. "We are members of John Morgan's Raiders, from the fair land of Kentucky," he announced to the surprised cashier. "Your village is now in the possession of the Confederate States Of America. We shall do to you what your Sheridan is doing to us." He butted the barrel of his Colt to Bishop's forehead and marched him toward the back room.

Clerk Martin Seymour had heard Collins' brief speech from the back room and he tried to close and lock the door on the intruders. The Rebels forced it open, knocked Seymour to the floor, and one robber began chocking him. "We are going to take your money," Collins shouted at him, "and if you resist, we will blow your brains out." Seymour, gasping for breath, promised he would not resist. Collins then made Seymour and Bishop stand side by side in the back room, raise their right hands, and pledge an allegiance to the Confederacy. While the two employees repeated Collins' words, local shop owner Samuel Breck entered the front door of the bank to deposit $393 into his account. The money was quickly taken from him, stuffed into the pocket of a white overcoat, and Breck was waltzed into the back room to join in the swearing in ceremony. Close on the heels of Breck was 13 year old Morris Roach, an errand boy, coming to deposit $210 for his employer. He was also shuffled into the back room and his money taken from him.

As three of the robbers stuffed their money bags with United States bonds and greenbacks, Collins held his revolver at Bishop's head, threatening to shoot if he didn't reveal where the bank notes and gold were stored. The robbers had found bags of silver coins in the vault — almost $2,000 worth — but with the paper money and bonds, they could only carry some $500 worth of silver. Bishop insisted that there was no more money, gold,or bonds in the bank, but he was lying. There was $9,000 stashed under the counter in the front room, $50,000 in U.S.-bonds, and $50,000 in bank notes, which the robbers didn't see, although the bonds and notes were stacked neatly in view on a shelf near the vault. Bishop concluded that they didn't see the notes and bonds because they were too nervous and smelled of alcohol, meaning that some of them were probably intoxicated. Collins kept shouting about the dastardly acts of Sherman and Sheridan as he prodded Bishop.

Then, they all heard gun fire from the street, and the robbers retreated, backing one at a time out the front door of the bank, each with a heavy leather satchel of valuables slung over his shoulder. Collins was the last one out, reminding them they had just sworn an allegiance to the Confederacy and were no longer citizens of the United States.

Lieutenant Bennett Young of the Confederacy's famous Morgan's Raiders, was the leader of this surprise attack on St. Albans. It had been months in the planning from bases in Montreal and at Phillipsburg, Quebec, in neutral Canada, 15 miles from St. Albans. Only 22 Confederate cavalrymen participated in the raid, not hundreds as the Raiders had announced. They entered the tiny yet prosperous Vermont village in twos and threes by train and coach, days before the attack, and lived incognito at various hotels and boarding houses on Main Street. The time for the Southerners to rise in the North was set days in advance — Three P.M., on Wednesday, the day after market day, when the street would be quiet, yet St. Alban's banks would be filled with money from the previous day's activities. The purpose of the mission was three-fold:(1) To repay in kind the alleged atrocities by Northern forces in the South (2) To help restore the depleated coffers of the Confederacy with Northern money; and (3), to panic American citizens on the Northern border, forcing U.S. troops in the South to be reassigned to Vermont to protect border towns from further attacks.

Poor Sarah Clark had been the pawn in Young's final planning stages. During his stroll with Sarah through Taylor Park, Young decided to use the park as his prisoner-of-war camp for holding local citizens, that they would corral from Main Street. It could be easily guarded by two of his cavalrymen. Quality horses could be obtained at the Governor's stables, which starry-eyed Sarah had revealed to Young during their tour. Stealing a few horses from the Governor was easy, but Young needed 22 of them for the get-away back into Canada. He decided that he would procure the needed remaining horses once the action began, at Field's and Fuller's Livery Stables on Main Street. Then he would burn down the stables as part of his plan to destroy St. Albans.

As Young and two of his men burst into the stables, Mr. Field knew immediately what their purpose was, and he hated horse thieves with a passion. He went for Young, who immediately shot at Field, the ball creasing his head and knocking off his hat. As one of the Rebels led seven horses out of the stables, Ed Fuller arrived and asked what was going on. "Keep quiet, or they'll shoot you", cried Field. Young laughed. "Is this a joke?" asked Fuller, but then seeing Young's Navy

Colt, he realized it wasn't. He quickly turned and ran for the house, but Young didn't shoot or follow. He busied himself with the others, getting the horses out onto the street. Fuller found an old rifle he kept in the house and walked back out the door to the stables. As Young came out, guiding more horses, Fuller aimed and fired, but nothing happened. Fuller pulled the trigger again, but there was just a clicking sound. He ran back into the house and reloaded, then as Young mounted one of the horses, he pulled the trigger again, and the rifle misfired again. Fuller cursed and threw the gun into a neaby field, and Young, not noticing him until the gun misfired for the third time, merely laughed, threw a fire bomb into the stables, and rode off with the others. Watching the horse thieves from behind a nearby tree, was a visitor from Manchester, New Hampshire, Mat Morrison. He tried to run across the street in front of the thieves to duck into Miss Beattie's Millinery Store, but Young saw him and fired. Morrison was hit in the stomach and he fell to the street. He died two days later.

Outside the First National Bank, McGrorty and his men, loaded down with money, heard the Rebel yells and shooting as Young headed up the street with the horses. McGrorty, however, was impatient so he started to mount a hitched horse by the side of the road. Out of Jaquez's Grocery Store came a tough Canadian trapper known as Frenchy Boivin. It was his horse, and no one was going to steal it from him. He jumped McGrorty as he sat in the saddle and wrestled him to the ground. Boivin was getting the best of the scrap, when another Rebel, Caleb Wallace jumped in to help McGrorty. Frenchy Boivin was holding his own against both of them, when a third Reb placed the barrel of his Colt against Frenchy's head. Frenchy let go of both men and was marched across Fairfield Street to Taylor Park, where he was held prisoner under two mounted Confederate guards. There were six other St. Albans residents coralled in the park as prisoners when Frenchy arrived. One was badly wounded, an elderly, well dressed man named Collins Huntington, who had been shot in the ribs by Young. Mr. Huntington, on the way down to meet his children at school, was ordered by Young to go to the green, where he was held prisoner. Huntington thought Young was a drunkin fool and told him so. "If you don't go over, I'll shoot you," Young shouted from his horse. "You won't shoot me," Huntington shouted over his shoulder as he walked toward the school, but Young did shoot him. Huntington was dragged over to   Taylor Park, bleeding profusely, but he later recovered.

Young quickly delivered the stolen horses to bank robbers McGrorty, Collins, and Hutchinson and their crews, but as Hutchinson was mounting his horse, someone fired at him from the second story window of a nearby building. The shot just grazed him and he wheeled his horse, planting a well aimed shot into the open window with his Colt. A rifle fell out the window and the man followed, sprawling across the wooden sidewalk.

Now it was time to burn down the town as Young had planned. He passed out some 40 firebombs to his men, and they galloped up and down Main Street, throwing them at doorways and into windows. The livery stables were already on fire, but now, the Atwood Building, the American House and lesser building were ablaze. Rebel yells filled the smoky air. It was only 3:20 p.m. and the Confederacy was in control of St. Albans.

A 19 year old boy was responsible for stopping Morgan's Raiders from making a complete destruction of the town. George Conger was a lieutenant in the Vermont Cavalry. Hearing the gunfire and seeing the smoke, he rallied the men working in the machine shops and at the railroad depot on Foundry Street, only a block from Main Street. Mounting his horse like Paul Revere, he raced up and down the streets, shouting, "The Rebels are here! Get your guns and head for Main Street!" As the men obeyed, Conger proceeded to set up a human road block of armed men across Main Street, where it led to the Sheldon Road and Canada. Young saw the defence forming and ordered his men to charge it. The villagers dispersed as the shouting, shooting cavalrymen attacked them, but Conger had them quickly reform. Young realized that someone with military training was now leading the St. Albans men. He had his Rebels attack the line of fire again, but this time he ordered them to keep on riding towards the village of Sheldon. One of the Rebels was wounded and almost fell off his horse as he broke through the defense, but not one Vermont man was hit. As the Rebels rode off, their stolen horses heavily burdened with satchels carrying over $208,000, Conger quickly assembled 15 armed men on horseback to ride after them.

The Rebels had not destroyed the village as planned, and at about the time they were forced to ride off, Jackson Clark and Marcus Beardsley were being let out of the stuffy Franklin County Bank vault. Although the gruff Confederate Raider, William Hutchinson, had promised them death by suffocation, he had left the key to the vault on the cashier's counter.

On the way to Sheldon, the Rebels burned a house and two barns, and although they attempted to burn down the bridge at Sheldon, blocking attempts of Conger's posse to follow them, they politely waited for a farmer with a wagon-load of hay to pass over the bridge before igniting it. Conger and his men arrived 15 minutes later and were in time to put out the fire, save the bridge and cross it. At Sheldon, the Rebels had planned to rob the Missisquoi Bank, but it was closed and they didn't have time nor the means to break in. It was obvious to Young that the Vermonters would soon be in hot pursuit, so he again divided his Raiders into small groups of two and three men, who took various routes into Canada. George Conger and his posse didn't stop at the border. They continued the chase into neutral Canada, even though he knew it might mean trouble from the British authorities, who seemed more sympathetic toward the Confederacy than toward the United States.

The next day, 14 of the Raiders were captured by Canadian authorities at and near Philipsburg. Hearing of the capture, Young, who was hiding out near Montreal, rode back to the border in hopes of rescuing his friends. At a farmhouse near Philipsburg, two days later, Conger and his men managed to corner Young and force him to surrender. Pleased at their easy catch, Conger's boys tied up the Rebel, threw him on a horse and headed back for Vermont, where they assured Bennett Young, he would hang. Conger, however, was stopped by a company of British Regulars before he managed to cross the border back into America. The British Major insisted that Young be turned over to him, and that within a few days, after undergoing Canadian legal procedure, Young and the other 14 captured Rebels, would be turned over to the American government. Conger reluctantly agreed to allow the British to have Young.

The trial of the captured Raiders was set for December 13th in Montreal. In the meantime, over 500 United States infantry, home guard and cavalry were placed in makeshift barracks at St. Albans to ward off further attacks by the Confederacy — it was like locking the barn door after the horses had fled. The third purpose of Bennett Young's mission into Vermont was working — the Yanks were taking fighting men from the war in the South to protect the Canadian border.

Some $80,000 of the stolen money was recaptured when Young and his compatriots were taken by the Canadians, and Vermont bankers were at the trial in Montreal, ready to take their money back to America. Federal Marshals and Vermont Sheriffs, handcuffs in hand, were there too, prepared to slap the cuffs onto the wrists of the guilty Rebels and return them to Vermont for hanging. The courtroom was crammed with Canadians, mostly Confederate supporters, and the room swelled with Rebel yells, as the Judge declared that, "this raid was an act of war, and I have no jurisdiction in the matter. Therefore," he announced, "I order the prisoners released, and the stolen money given back to them."

Bennet Young smiled and waved at the bankers, marshalls, and sheriffs and left the courtroom a free man. He stayed a bit longer in Canada to study law, and then saw to it that the $208,000 in stolen money was turned over to Confederate President Jefferson Davis. He also took time out to write Sarah Clark a nice letter explaining everything, and asking her if she'd send him copies of the Vermont Daily Messenger, detailing the Raid. Bennett Young was a Southern gentleman, and Sarah had to smile at his polite boldness. He had even enclosed $3.00 with the letter for the newspapers.

After the war, Young became a successful lawyer in his hometown of Louisville, Kentucky, and later President of the Southern Railroad. Some forty years after the Raid, he was asked by St. Albans citizens to come back to Vermont to lead a band of Rebels in a reenactment of the Raid for the town's Centennial. He accepted the offer, but the Grand Army of the Republic, made up of Civil War Northern veterans, objected, and Bennett Young thought it wiser not to travel to Vermont.

The closest he ever got to St. Albans again was in 1911, when he and his wife and daughter, visited Montreal. A group of St. Albans citizens, two of whom were present during the Raid, visited him there. When they asked the 68 year old man what his thoughts were about his bold attack on the town, he answered, "It was merely a reckless escapade of a flaming youth of twenty one, steeped in the patriotism of the South. In reflection," he said, "I wonder how I ever undertook it . . . I am now as loyal to my reunited country as I was then to my cherished Confederacy."

Bennet Young died in Kentucky on February 23, 1919, age 76.

Saint Albans, Vermont's Main Street, a few days after the Raid, and captured Rebels in Canada. Sitting left, is William Hutchinson, and sitting on the right is Rebel Leader, Bennett Young. *Photos courtesy of the Library of Congress.*

V
AMERICA NEEDED A HERO

A low-lying mist dampened the dense Argonne Forest on the morning of October 8, 1918. There was neither sound nor movement in the woods,yet the Yanks who were about to enter it knew that over four hundred thousand enemy were there, waiting and watching. German mortars had bombarded the American trenches throughout the evening and young Bill Cutting laid in the cold mud, listening to screams of agony as his comrades were blown to pieces. He found it impossible to sleep. Today would be the thirteenth day of the bloody battle of the Meuse-Argonne. Unlucky thirteen, thought Cutting, and when we enter the forest the Germans are sure to make a last ditch defensive. Bill's stomach knotted. If he died this day, no one would know what happened to him. The thought frightened him.

Standing near Bill in the trench, waiting for the signal to attack, was his good friend and platoon leader, Bernie Early from Connecticut. Bill wondered if he should reveal his long-kept secret to Bernie. As he slid across the muddy embankment, edging his way to Sergeant Early's side, he started thinking about his mother and other folks back in Brookline, Massachusetts.

"Otis," the neighborhood kids called him, "Oh Otis", they would razz the skinny red-head. He would chase after them in a rage, but they'd dodge around him yelling, "What's the matter O--tis, can't you catch us?" Bill smiled to himself as he remembered the few he had caught and whipped down to size. "Otis, Otis Merrithew," he mumbled under his breath and cringed at the sound of his real name. Actually, the name Otis was one to be proud of. He had been named after a famous ancestor, James Otis, a Boston hero of the American Revolution.

At the age of nineteen, Otis Merrithew ran away from home to join the Army. On his way to the recruiting station in Boston, he noticed a billboard outside a clothing store displaying the name "William B. Cutting". A good rugged name for a soldier thought Otis, and he immediately adopted it as his own.

"Bernie," said Bill, tapping his friend on the shoulder, "I've got something to tell you. . ."

Bernie Early looked at Bill, then at his wristwatch. It was 6:00 am. "Charge!" he shouted into Bill Cutting's ear. The crackling of machine gun and rifle bullets shattered the morning silence. Up and over the top went Company G of the 82 Division, "The All American Division" of the 328th Infantry. Bill Cutting heard men shout, some with hate, some with hidden fear as they stumbled on, others with pain as they toppled back into the trenches. Bill quickly assembled the five men of his squad and led them across a field toward the crest of Hill 223, just north of Chatel Chehery, where the Company would assemble for the main assault. Corporal Murray Savage and his squad were on Bill's right and Corporal Alvin York with his five privates were rushing up the hill on Bill's left. Cutting was a bit fearful of York, for he recalled that during a previous attack York had jumped up on a parapet and shouted, "I want to go home, for God's sake, why isn't this war over?" Sergeant Early had rushed up to the tall Tennesseean and pointing a pistol at his forehead he shouted, "If you don't shut up, I'll blow your brains out." York had seemed to come around after that episode, but Bill still didn't trust him.

Bullets were whizzing all around them, and although the Yanks could not see the enemy, they could see the sparks of machine gun fire spitting out of the misty forest. One of Savage's men fell, then Bill saw one of his own men hit the ground. As Company G reached the top of the hill, the Germans sent over a barrage of gas. The doughboys quickly slipped on their masks, but those who weren't quick enough suffered an agonizing death. The Yanks could advance no further. They were smothered by gas and pinned down to the crest of Hill 223 by machine gun fire.

Sergeant Early was chosen to pick a detail of 16 men to approach the enemy lines from the left flank in an attempt to knock out as many machine gun nests as possible and to cut off their supply lines. Early selected Savage, Cutting, York and their squads to accompany him. The 17 men circled Hill 223 to a point about a quarter of a mile from where Company G was bogged down. Early led them across a field of rifle fire and maneuvered them into the woods. Shielding themselves in the underbrush, they passed unnoticed through the German's second line of defense, then followed an unoccupied trench and scattered into the woods.

Sergeant Early hoped to attack the machine guns covering Hill 223 from the rear, but he was now uncertain of his own position. Thus far the mist had helped to conceal the movements of this special detail, but now the sun was shining through the trees burning off the mist. The Sergeant ordered his men to circle back towards the front lines and as they proceeded cautiously down a winding dirt path, they spotted two Germans up ahead, both were wearing Red Cross arm bands. When the Germans spied the Yanks, they ran. One fell, got up again, and quickly followed his friend into the forest. Early commanded them to hault, but they kept going. "We've got to kill or capture those two," shouted Early, "if not, they'll expose our position." The doughboys dispersed into the woods and raced through the underbrush on the heels of the two Germans.

"We've lost them," reported Bill Cutting, doubling back to rejoin his platoon sergeant, "but the boys have found something more interesting in a clearing up ahead, a group of Germans just sitting around a campfire gabbing. It must be an enemy headquarters." Early followed Cutting through the woods to the edge of the clearing. It was a Battalion Headquarters, Early concluded, with over 30 soldiers gathered together in council. Sergeant Early concealed his men in the bushes around the clearing. Then he gave the command to fire. In the first blast, fifteen to eighteen Germans fell, mortally wounded. The survivors fell to their knees crying "Kamarad, Kamarad," which the Yanks recognized as a sign of surrender. "This is murder, cease firing," shouted Early stepping into the clearing. "Let's get these Germans out of here, on the double."

The Sergeant ordered Corporal York and his squad to remain concealed, as Corporal Savage and Cutting with their squads lined up the prisoners in a column of twos and collected their fire arms. A German Major was in command, and as Sergeant Early confronted him, someone on a nearby hillside shouted a command. The entire column of prisoners fell flat on their stomachs, and all hell broke loose. Machine gun bullets whistled through the air and grenades were lobbed from the hillside into the clearing. Sergeant Early was punctured with six bullet holes in the back. Cutting received five in his left arm and Savage was blown to bits by a grenade. Cutting's squad was mowed down, as were all but one of Savage's. York and his five men, well hidden in the shrubs, could not be seen by the enemy. Bill Cutting and Private Mario Muzzi, who was also wounded, managed to crawl into the bushes and started firing back. There were so many machine guns firing down on them, Cutting and Muzzi didn't know where the bullets were coming from. Some of the Germans lying on the ground went for their weapons and the remaining Yanks started picking them off. Then there came a lull in the firing. On the hillside, running along a 40-yard crest was a battalion of German machine gunners with 35 gun muzzles pointing into the clearing. They waited for some movement in the bushes below. One of the Yanks lying in the clearing raised his head. It was Early. "Cutting, Cutting," he moaned, "help me,. . . take over and get us out of here."

A few of the German machine gunners peeked over their pits to see what was going on. York spied them and with three quick shots, sent three bodies tumbling down the hill. Two German grenades came bouncing into the clearing and exploded, destroying four of the unarmed Germans who were lying with their faces in the dirt.

Guessing that there were only a handful of Americans left below, seven Germans, led by an officer, came running down the hill, their rifles blazing. They headed for Sergeant York. The boy from Tennessee, who had been weaned on a hunting rifle, plucked off all seven. The German lieutenant landed no more than ten feet away from York's rifle barrel. In the meantime, Corporal Cutting had warned the German Major lying on the ground that if the machine guns didn't cease firing and the gunners didn't surrender, he would personally "knock off every German prisoner lying on the ground." The German Major took a little silver whistle from his pocket and blew it. "We give up. We've had enough," he cried in broken English. The firing stopped and York shouted, "Come on down with your hands in the air." Like rodents summoned by the piper's tune, ninety Germans threw down their arms and came out from behind the trees and over the crest of the hill. The ten Yanks who were left standing came out of their hiding places and Cutting, with blood gushing from his left arm, ordered the German Major to turn over his Luger, which he did. Then Cutting once again lined up the prisoners in columns of twos and had them counted. They had 110 German captives, including three officers. There were 25 Germans lying on the ground, killed in the battle. A make shift stretcher was made for Sergeant Early and the unique parade of prisoners, guarded by ten American doughboys, headed for the front lines.

Bill Cutting led the prisoners through thickly wooded areas, for not only was the detail in danger of German guns, but of American fire as well. As they approached the German front-line trenches, Cutting ordered the German Major to have all the gunners facing Hill 223 surrender, and if they failed to do so, the prisoners would die. The Major shouted to the men in the trenches and they came out with their hands in the air. Bill Cutting took another count. He now had 132 prisoners. Then he saw, about 125 yards away, his own Battalion Adjutant, Lieutenant Charles Woods, and Sergeant Harry Parsons coming towards them. The rest of the American command was about to enter the woods, but instead they came rushing toward the ten Yanks and their prisoners. "What you got there," shouted Lieutenant Woods, "the whole damned German Army?" A wild cheer went up from Company G and Sergeant Harry Parsons ran up to Bill Cutting and shook his right hand like a well pump. Then Parsons looked at Bill's helmet and saw three bullet holes in it. He pulled the helmet off Bill's head and shouted,

"Cutting, you're hit."

"No, not there, but I have a flesh wound here," said Bill pointing to his left arm. Parsons tried to pull Cutting out of line to give him first aid. "To hell with first aid, look at the souvenir I have," said Bill holding up a German Luger.

"Never mind that," said Parson, "you're bleeding like a stuffed pig."

After talking briefly with the German Major, Lieutenant Woods asked who was next in command and Corporal York stepped forward. Woods then detailed another squad to assist York and his squad to march the prisoners back to Division Headquarters.

In the first aid shanty, Parsons bandaged Cutting's arm, then started laughing. "You're the luckiest guy I know," he said holding up Cutting's knapsack, "not only did you get three bullets in your helmet, but you got two more in your back pack that were stopped by a can of corned beef."

Cutting looked at the can that was split wide open and shook his head. "I guess I was lucky, but now I've got to get back to my prisoners."

"Oh no you don't," said Parsons. "That hole in your arm isn't just a flesh wound. You need hospital treatment and Lieutenant Woods gave me orders for you to climb into one of those ambulances outside." Cutting reluctantly agreed. Three ambulances were waiting near the shanty. One carried Sergeant Early and the second carried three wounded Germans. "Come to think of it," said Cutting, jumping into the front seat of the third sedan, "I could use a rest." That's the last anyone saw or head of Bill Cutting for eleven years.

After the five bullets were removed from Cutting's left arm, he had plenty of time to relax in the hospital. He slept and read and was content with his lot in life, until two weeks after the battle when he picked up a copy of the Stars & Stripes carrying the headline "Sergeant York-Hero of Argonne Forest." "York?" shouted Bill Cutting aloud. "What about the other sixteen men? If there was a hero, it was Bernie Early and no one else." The men in the ward tried to quiet Bill, but he was furious, as were the other living members of the detail who were with York that day. Most of them had returned to the front and hadn't heard for weeks later that York was the champion of World War I.

The boys had remembered York as a quiet guy who continually

moaned over his "gal friend" back home at the Valley of the Three Forks O' the Wolf. York was never one to brag about or exploit his battle achievements, and during boot training at Camp Gordon he was in jail more than he was out, not because he was wild but because he objected to war. Back home in the mountains of Tennessee, the local church pastor and Mrs. York tried to exempt Alvin from the Army on religious principals, but the draft board persuaded him to serve his country, guaranteeing that he would not have to fight. But at Camp Gordon he was taught to kill other human beings and he rebelled. York was then given the chance to become a member of a color guard, but he could not comprehend the assignment and he was made a line corporal. Although he hesitated at killing Germans in battles prior to the fight in the Argonne Forest, he was, without doubt, a hero in the forest, but not the only hero. Alvin York, however, was not the cause of this misrepresentation; he was the victim of it.

America needed a hero. The front line newspaper and magazine reporters hungered, as did the people back home, for news of American gallantry in World War I. Between the Spring of 1917 and the autumn of 1918, over two million Yanks boarded troop ships for France. The boys spent almost a year "over there" training for trench warfare and then they had to wait for a few more months for their initial clash with the enemy. Even in late 1918, when news of the first great battles between Yanks and Germans filtered across the Atlantic, the information was spotty and too general in content to satisfy the folks back home. They had been listening to war slogans and songs until they were red, white, and blue in the face. They wanted and felt deserving of a doughboy hero to worship.

When Alvin York came marching into division headquarters with 132 prisoners, he was surrounded by reporters. "Who captured all these German?" asked George Palluto of the Saturday Evening Post.

"York's in command," replied one of the privates. York, being a quiet sort of guy, didn't have much to say, so the newspaper and magazine reporters said it for him. They contributed his silence to modesty, and so the legend began.

There was no stopping the publicity and honors York received, and when the Tennesseean got around to telling reporters that he didn't do it alone, he was cheered and praised for his modesty. He was upped in rank to sergeant; General John Pershing pinned the Congressional Medal of Honor on his chest, the highest award for valor that the United States government bestows; and French Marshal Foch presented York with the Croix de Guerre with Palm. He received the Distinguished Service Cross, the Medaille Militaire, Italy's War Cross, and other medals. England was the only ally that did not bestow a medal on him. The Prince of Wales stated that if America could prove that York did what was said of him, the sergeant would receive the Victoria Cross, but this was one medal Alvin did not get.

He never returned to his outfit but instead toured Europe and then boarded a supply ship back to the States. When his ship landed in New York in the Spring of 1919, waiting Americans threw roses at his feet. He was snatched away from the other returning veterans and escorted to a massive banquet where he was presented $2,000 in Liberty Bonds, more than he could make in three years working in the Tennessee Mountains. He was placed on the Army's Retirement list with pay for life, and by popular subscription, was given a farm in his home state with livestock, furnishings, and more acreage than he'd ever know what to do with. He was offered a multitude of positions with glowing salaries,and many companies wanted to name products after him, but Alvin turned down all offers of position.

He retired to the land of the Hatfields and the McCoys, returning to his widow mother and her brood of eleven children in an old two-room shanty at the Valley of the Three Forks O' the Wolf. When he was approached by publishers to have books written about him, he said he wouldn't mind if they were done right but each and every one of them, when published, was steeped with exaggeration. It was no longer Cutting who led the prisoners out of the forest and it was no longer Early who maneuvered them into the forest. It was York. It was York who forced the Germans to surrender as the other members of the detail stood by helplessly, and then Ripley in his "Believe It Or Not" added the magic word, "single-handed" and everyone, except the men who were with York, believed Ripley. When writers asked the men who were in York's detail to supply sworn affidavits of the Tennessean's heroism, only three of the ten replied with favorable comments,and those three were members of York's own squad. Alvin did leave Tennessee to tour the country for a few months, but hesitated at entering cities where living members of the special detail lived.

He returned to the mountains, married his childhood sweetheart and tried to quietly live out his life. When the remaining members of Early's detail returned to the states months after York returned, they decided to look up Bernie Early and Bill Cutting to help them fight the falsehoods that York's promoters initiated. Early, who had made a miraculous recovery after the six bullets were removed from his back, was willing, but he needed the help of Cutting who had taken command during the battle. Early searched everywhere for Bill Cutting and even traveled to Boston and Brookline, Massachusetts in his effort to trace him, but the Army had no record of a Bill Cutting. The Veterans Administration told Bernie that a Bill Cutting never served in the United States Army during the war. Early knew different and after calling on every Cutting in the Boston area, he returned to Connecticut, weary and puzzled, but still willing to fight for the recognition due him and his men.

In October of 1929, eleven years after the battle, the Army decided to have a reunion of "York's" special detail in Washington, D.C. The Department of the Army realized that there was an undercurrent of resentment from some of the men who served with York and they hoped this reunion would help smooth things over. "A re-enactment of the great battle" was the theme of the meeting and although there was not a re-enactment of the old battle at the meeting, all the survivors showed up — there was a new battle brewing.

When Bill Cutting walked into the room, no one, especially Bernie Early, could believe his eyes. They had all concluded, since they could not find a trace of Bill, that he had died from his wounds in France. Bill had read about the reunion in the newspapers. After being welcomed by his buddies, he explained to them the reason why no one could find him. He had used an alias while serving the Army and when he returned home after the war, his mother marched him down to the Veterans Administration Office and made him change all his military records to read his real name, Otis Merrithew, instead of Bill Cutting.

Alvin York, of course, was at the reunion, but only four of the ten survivors even said hello to him. The remaining men cornered the Army officers and Washington officials who were on hand and told them what really happened in the Argonne Forest. The conversations became heated when the men were told that Congress was presently passing a bill stating that medals would no longer be presented to World War I veterans. The party broke up early with the various factions going their own way, but Bernie Early decided to stay in Washington and "fight this thing to the end." He finally won his personal battle and received the Distinguished Service Cross before the year was out. Early also recommended Otis Merrithew for the D.S.C., as did a well-known Senator and an Army Major, but Otis did not receive his medal.

Otis Merrithew returned to his wife and two daughters in Brookline and tried to forget the issue. "History was made,"he said, "and nothing was going to change it." But in 1941, something did make Otis change his mind about fighting the issue. A representative of Warner Brothers Studios came to Merrithew's door one morning, offering him $250 if he would sign his name to an agreement to use his name in a movie being made about Sergeant York. Otis told the man to "get out." "They'll just make the picture without using your name," said the man, "and believe me, it's not Warner Brothers that wants to make the picture — it's the War Department."

"Okay," said Otis. "You can use my name, but that movie had better be accurate." The man smiled and left. Otis saw the movie three times,and each time he was tempted to throw something at the screen. Gary Cooper, portraying Sergeant York, had won the battle "single-handedly," and unlike their thankful counterparts in the movie, the real survivors of the battle were furious.

On January 4, 1942, a feature article was published in the Bridgeport, Connecticut Sunday Herald with the headline, "YORK PHONY HERO . . ." The article was made up of quotes from a battlescarred, gassed veteran of the war named Arthur Ward. He had served 14 months in France with York. "Ask the vets about York," said Ward. "He's yellow and I'd tell him right to his face. Any and all honors Sergeant York has been lapping up all over the country belong to Otis Merrithew." Merrithew began writing letters to his Congressmen, to the War Department,and to the President of the United States. He wrote to every President through Eisenhower, then he gave up, but his family kept up the battle for him. In the Spring of 1963, Otis Merrithew's grand-daughter, Joanne Fay, age twelve, wrote to President John F. Kennedy, stating that she knew of only two famous men who were born and brought up in Brookline, Massachusetts; "you and my grandfather." Her charming letter brought action from President Kennedy, and on July 25, 1963, Congress amended the law disallowing further medals to World War I veterans.

It was two years later that Otis got official word, per order of President Lyndon Johnson, that he was to be awarded the "Silver Star" for bravery at Fort Devens, Massachusetts, on October 21, 1965. Otis had waited 47 years to receive the recognition and glory due him. It was one year since Sergeant York had died a pauper in the Tennessee Hills, and on that day, Otis had flown the flag in front of his Brookline home at half-mast.

The 68 year-old Otis Merrithew, still lean, strong and chipper, was picked up at his home by an Army limosine, and his family and friends were also driven to Fort Devens by the military. He stood before the Army Generals and 100 guests, including ten of his grandchildren, as the long awaited medal was pinned to his chest. It was his proudest day - his eyes were moist and his voice quivered as he spoke: "Many good Americans have died fighting for this country," he said, "and there was one guy in my outfit who was a conscientious objector - but once he was in the thick of battle, he fought like a true American, and almost captured the whole damned German Army singled-handed. His name was Alvin York, and he was a hero."

Otis Merrithew of Brookline, MA, holds painting of hero Bill Cutting. Photo by George Dow. World War I heros, eleven years after the war: (1) Pvt. Patrick Donahue; (2) Otis Merrithew and family; (3.) Pvt. Mario Muzzi; (4.) Pvt. George Willis; (5.) Pvt. Michael Sacina; (6.) Sgt. Bernard Early and wife; (7.) Sgt. Harry Parsons.

*Ink sketch on parchment of **Russian** refugees during World War II, by Andris Bezdomini. The sketch somehow survived the concentration camps.*

VI
THE QUIET CONNECTICUT YANKEE

In the early 1960's, fresh out of college and a two-year stint in the Army, I managed to find a job in my chosen field as a copywriter for an advertising firm in Connecticut. One of my first assignments was to work with an artist in developing an employee recruiting brochure for a major Hartford insurance company. The artist was a tall, thin, quiet man in his late forties. He was cordial enough, but during the many days we worked together, he hardly said a word beyond discussing the technicalities of the job. One day, I asked him to join me at lunch.

"I'm starved," I commented off-handedly as we entered the cafeteria together.

"Please," he said in all seriousness, patting my shoulder, "never say that, for you don't know what starving is . . ."

Among the 1,000 Ukrainians exiled to Siberia in 1914, who were accused of being anti-Russian sympathizers, was Andris Bezdomini. His father, Stive, was a politician in a small Ukrainian town, and the Czar believed that Stive was siding with the Austro-Hungarians in their heated cold war with the Russians. Stive Bezdomini, his wife, daughter, and son Andris were forced to leave all possessions behind as they were loaded into a horse-drawn cart and transported forty miles through the snow to a waiting freight train. The Bezdominis were crowded together with other families on the floor of a box-car. The car door was bolted shut, and the prisoners huddled together to keep warm. Andris remembers nothing of the long, sullen journey to the freezing wastelands of Russia, for he was only a year old at the time.

For seven years the Bezdominis lived with five other families in one of the decaying, unheated barracks of Siberia. Stive and his wife worked day and night in a factory. The children grew up in a dismal world of nine-month long winters, each winter day revealing only three hours of sunlight.

In 1921, the new communist regime gave Stive the choice of remaining in Siberia or returning to his homeland to become a Russian or Polish citizen. The communists had taken over Ukrainia and it was under Polish control. A nation had been forced to swallow its pride. Stive did the same and returned home with his family, a Polish citizen. To Andris, this new life was wonderful; the days were longer, the winters shorter, and he was allowed to enter school. But, his parents were unhappy. They could see through the teachings of Marx and Lenin, and they had seen the communist police destroy churches and arrest priests. This wasn't their idea of freedom.

Andris was a good student and showed exceptional talent in drawing. A teacher suggested that he show some of his creations to the noted artist Gey Bay, who ran an art school in Odessa on the Black Sea. Andris went to see the famous artist. Gey Bay, a bull of a man with bushy beard and smiling eyes, took a liking to the teenager and saw that the boy had talent.

"You must complete high school before you study art," stated the master, "but, if you paint one picture a day until you graduate, I will see to it that you receive a scholarship to the art school."

Andris agreed, but this would be quite a task for the boy who had to walk fourteen miles to and from high school every day. Andris kept his promise to the great Gey Bay who, in turn, upheld his end of the bargain. The master was pleased with the progress of the young artist and soon, they were working together, painting holy pictures on the interior walls of churches. At the time, painting churches was a lucrative business in Poland. Upon completing art school, Andris rented a room in the big city and set up his own studio.

Early on the morning of September 1, 1939, Andris left his studio to make some finishing touches on a church painting in a nearby town. It was a warm autumn day, and Andris walked leisurely down the road wearing only a thin pair of slacks and a T-shirt. He worked diligently through the morning. It was only a few minutes past the noon hour when he heard the warning whistle and the clatter and chatter of people running for shelter outside the church. He completed his work while his paints were usable, then gathered together his brushes and pallette. Outside, everything was dead silent, not a person was in sight. Then he heard the eerie whine overhead, the delayed screams and the explosions that shook the earth around him. He ran to the shelter, dodging the spray of concrete and metal, down the stairway and into the damp cellar. He remained in the shelter with the townspeople for the rest of the day. When the all-clear signal was given, he trudged back to the city, shivering in his thin attire. When he arrived at his studio, he found it completely demolished. His art work, his clothes, everything, destroyed by a German bomb.

For the next three days, Andris, wearing his only pair of slacks and T-shirt, walked almost 100 miles to the home of his parents. Germany and Poland were at war, but to Andris and his father this wasn't the most pressing problem and worry. At the outbreak of the war, the Russians immediately occupied the Ukrainian territory and, as usual, placed many of the Ukrainians under arrest for suspicion of treason. The Russians established their own government in the territory and deprived the people of their property. The Ukrainins tried to hide their dislike for the Russians, but as the arrests became more frequent, some of the bolder Ukrainians, like Stive and Andris Bezdomini, spoke out in protest. Andris saw the Russian police come after his best friend, Nicholas Gatzi. The young man tried to escape over a frozen pond behind his home, but the police caught him and shot him three times through the head. Andris had loved the happy-go-lucky Gatzi, and he cried over his loss for days. Then, however, the Russians came for Stive and Andris.

Andris remembers that snowy evening of March 9, 1940 very well, for it was the last time he saw his family. His mother and sister were to go with a neighbor to a different town where they would adopt new names. Andris was to go his separate way alone. Stive would stay and keep the Russian police occupied at his home. Andris Bezdomini protested, but Stive wasn't going to have his family return to the nightmares of Siberia. "I am old," said his father, "I have lived my life. you at least must be given a chance to live yours."

His mother would go to protect her daughter. Two women alone would have a better chance of escape than if they were with a man, especially with Andris who was known as an anti-Communist. "You go, I will die after three years," cried his 65 year old mother. Andris dressed warmly and walked out the back door of the house. He didn't turn around, he just walked aimlessly through the fields. He didn't know where he was going and, at the time, he didn't care. Through the efforts of the townspeople, his mother and sister successfully escaped to another town. His father was handcuffed and under armed guard was transported once again to Siberia.

Andris walked for four days until he found work in a big city as a bookkeeper in a shoe factory. He changed his name and made no attempt to develop new friends. Andris was at the factory only a few months when two Russian newpaper reporters came to see a fellow worker. They had a previously written article with them. The article praised the life of a working man under communism. "Sign your name to this," stated one off the reporters to the aging factory worker.

"But I didn't write it," said the worker.

The reporter looked coldly at the old man, "Well, isn't everything that is written here true?"

The worker said nothing, he knew what would happen to him if he did. He signed his name at the bottom of the article and walked off.

Andris decided it was time to move on. He adopted another alias and moved to another city. He found a job in a Russian furniture factory. Every night there were Communist meetings after work. If an employee did not attend the meetings, he was not only fired, but arrested and never heard from again. Andris kept moving towards the West and what he hoped was freedom. In one year he moved to five different cities, changing his name and occupation at each new location.

On June 21, 1941, he strolled into a Polish city near the western border and found a job in a retail shop under one of his aliases. On that same day, another stranger entered the city — the German army. Andris had found a room, worked for a day, and walked up to a nearby hill for a stretch of the legs before his evening meal. From his perch, he could see people running in the distance. They were Russian soldiers. Then he heard the repeating thud of machine gun bullets, and the men in uniform fell to the ground. Andris was excited. He started running down the hill towards the city. Then he spied a machine gun muzzle following his movements from a nearby bush. He froze, his heart pounding. "I am not a Russian," shouted Andris in German. "I am just walking back to town to eat supper."

There was no reply from the German soldiers crouched behind the bush. A plane flying over the hill came into Andris' line of vision. It was sweeping in for an attack. The German soldiers motioned Andris to hit the dirt, and he did so as the plane zoomed in, fired a few shots, and climbed back into the clouds. The Germans walked over to Andris. At first, the Ukrainian was frightened, but the Germans were friendly and impressed with how well he spoke their language. Andris also spoke Russian and Polish fluently, so the German Army employed him as an interpretor. He worked for them until March 9, 1943, the day that the Russians weakened the German stronghold on the Polish city. The Nazis were forced to retreat. Andris was loaded onto a truck with Polish prisoners and transported to Romania. He spent three months in a camp there, until the camp became over-crowded. He was then transfered to a camp in Hungary and from there, to another in Vienna, Austria.

Up to this time conditions in the German camps were not exceptionally bad, no one went hungry, but all camps were overcrowded. Some 1800 prisoners, including Andris, were moved from Vienna by train to a camp on the French border. When they arrived, the French camp was so overloaded with prisoners that the 1800 were sent back to Vienna where 400,000 prisoners were corraled in an open field. Two weeks later, the original 1800 were put aboard another train bound for a camp in Bavaria. On the second evening of travel, the freight train was bombed. The prisoners, heavily guarded, were taken off the train and allowed to sleep in the forest.

As they were about to board the train in the morning, Andris witnessed a tragic scene. A young girl was being separated from her parents by the Gestapo. The aging couple were crying and screaming in Russian at the German officers. Andris, thinking that the German's didn't understand the couple, went to their assistance. Speaking both Russian and German, Andris pleaded with the Gestapo to allow the teenaged girl to go with her parents. Andris was immediately kicked to the ground and beaten severely with rifle butts. Then, instead of being allowed to reboard the train, he was loaded onto a truck which he knew was heading for a German punishment camp located a few miles outside Nuremberg, Germany. He had heard people mention how awful German punishment camps were, but he couldn't possibly forsee how terrible they really were until he arrived at his hell-on-earth destination.

The huge, dismal camp was surrounded by an electric wire fence. Within this high-voltage barrier were wooden garages used as makeshift barracks for the prisoners. Everyone slept on concrete floors, approximately fifty people crammed together in each barrack. Three miles from these ugly quarters was an underground factory. It was like a city under the earth where the prisoners produced and distributed ammunition for the German front lines. It was here that Polish, French, English and Italian men and women worked day and night unwillingly for the German war effort. Prisoners walked three miles to work, through mud and snow, in wooden shoes provided by the captors. They began work at 6 a.m. each day, and there was nothing to eat until 12 noon, when fifteen minutes were alloted for them to each swallow down a rotten cabbage leaf and a bowl of warm water. The next break came at 6:00 p.m., when each prisoner received two potatoes. After eating these, everyone returned to work until 12 midnight. Many of them took their last steps on earth during the chilly, three-mile trudge to the damp barracks in the wee hours of the morning. None of the prisoners talked to each other, they were all too weak, but once in a while, someone would mumble something in his native tongue only to break the deathly silence. The smells in the barracks were almost unbearable. The nauseating stench of unclean bodies, people being sick and people being dead was nightmarish to come back to each evening and to wake up to each morning. Each day, before dawn when Andris entered the open building used as a makeshift toilet, he would find from five to ten people dead on the floor. Suicide was common, and many who could no longer endure the pangs of hunger would throw themselves against the high voltage electric fence. Anyone who was too weak to work was taken aside by a German guard and shot.

Everything was blurry and all colors faded into a dreary gray. After two months, this was the effect of hunger on Andris' eyesight. Many of the starving prisoners went blind, but as long as they could work, they weren't murdered by the Germans. One day, after four months of hard labor in the camp, Andris found a rotten apple in the mud on his way to work. He wolfed it down and, for an instant, his eyesight returned to normal. For a second, the surrounding landscape came into clear view. Andris thought of nothing but food from morning to night. He tried, but couldn't think of another thing. His fellow prisoners, he knew, were thinking the same; they would kill for a morsel of bread or a rotten potato. If there was one thing that Andris wanted more than anything in the world, it was a fresh potato. The potato became an obsession with him.

One morning, the young Frenchman who slept beside Andris became so violently ill that he couldn't walk. Andris tried to help, but he didn't have the energy to lift the man. If anyone was a second late when the whistle blew in the morning, he would go without food for three days. The Frenchman tried to make it, but couldn't. He was beaten by the German guards and left behind to die, but after his beating, the Frenchman stimulated enough energy to wobble into the prison yard and throw himself onto the electric fence. Andris estimated that twenty or more prisoners would die in this manner each day. But the number of prisoners in the camp never diminished, for forty to fifty new people would come into the camp each day to replace the dead.

One day, a heavy piece of ammunition slipped out of Andris' arms as he was loading it onto a truck. If fell on his foot, cracking the wooden shoe and splintering a bone. His leg began to swell and the pain was almost unbearable when he walked, but he dared not mention his suffering to the guards for fear of being shot. For the same reason, he tried not to limp when he walked. He worked on, sometimes wondering if he was going to live through the day, sometimes not caring if he did.

After six months, Andris was but a walking skeleton. He went about his work and his suffering silently until one day when a German woman, who worked in the factory but was not a prisoner, spoke to him:

"Where are you from?" she asked.

"Russia," he replied.

She then informed Andris that her husband was a prisoner in Russia. "I will help you," she stated, "in hopes that someone in Russia will help my husband."

The woman never spoke to Andris again, but every day she hid a piece of bread under a cart in the factory for Andris. Andris believes that this is what kept him alive during his remaining months in the prison camp. One time, she left a three pound loaf of black bread for the hungry Ukrainian. He gulped it down as fast as he could stuff it into his mouth, but at this stage of hunger, he was so dazed and bewildered that he didn't remember eating the bread. Two minutes after he had swallowed it, he began looking for it again and thought surely he had lost it or someone had stolen it. Ten minutes later he knew that he must have eaten it because he became very sick.

On April 17, 1945, the Americans came. The G.I.'s rolled into camp with truckloads of food which they tossed to the starving prisoners. They could have all they wanted to eat. The next morning, over one-third of the liberated prisoners were dead from overeating. Andris had previously read that a starving person could die from overeating, so he ate very little and controlled the great desire to eat more and more. Every person in the camp was given a clean American Army uniform to wear, including fatigue cap. Andris, in appearance, was a corporal in the U.S. Army. He was taken to the city of Nuremberg and given a room with bath, plus free meals at the U.S. Army mess. "The best food I ever tasted," was Andris' daily comment at the mess, a statement which raised a few G.I. eyebrows. Andris felt he was being treated like a king, or comparably, like a U.S. Army corporal, and he decided that he wanted to come to America. He almost changed his mind one day, however, when he received a severe tongue-lashing from a young Army lieutenant. Andris had merely passed by the young man on the street, said "hello" and walked on. The lieutenant marched Andris off to the Provost Martial, who cleared up the situation. The embarrassed lieutenant apologized to Andris, and Andris, in his spanking new corporal's uniform, apologized for not saluting the lieutenant.

Andris began painting again. He sold his art work on the street corners to American servicemen for cartons of cigarettes. With the cigarettes he would pay his rent, buy food and have plenty left over to sell to the Germans to gain extra spending money. There were many Ukrainians, Czechs, and Poles in Germany, all unwilling to return to their homeland. Andris made plans to come to America. A distant relative who lived in Massachusetts agreed to sponsor him. He was elated at gaining entrance to the land of the free, but sad at the thought he would never see his homeland again.

Andris lived in Massachusetts for one month and then decided that he wanted to live in a big city. He moved to Hartford, Connecticut, but had difficulty finding a job mainly because he knew only a few words of English. After walking the pavement for a few days, he found employment as a dishwasher in a local restaurant. He rented a room in a boarding house and, each night, he would return to his room to study English. As the Christmas season aproached, Andris was stimulated into painting the three cooks he worked with, depicted as the three Wise Men riding camels. The manager of the restaurant saw the painting and was so impressed that he hung it in the street window. This was his mistake, for it resulted in the loss of a fine dishwasher. Two accomplished Connecticut artists spied the painting and persuaded Andris to resume his art career. Andris left the dishes in the sink and, through the influence of these two men, was enrolled in a New York art school.

During his four years of study, Andris found time to continue his English language studies and to write three letters a week to his mother and sister, in hope that they might still be alive. He just couldn't give up hope. Upon graduation from art school, he returned to Hartford to become art director of an advertising firm and to marry a pretty Connecticut girl.

For five years he had been writing home to Russia without receiving one letter in return. When it finally came, he could hardly believe his eyes — it was in his mother's handwriting. As he tore open the envelope, he laughed and cried. It was a very short letter from his mother. She and her daughter had been captured by the Russians and had lived eight years in Siberia. They were then allowed to return home. Stive Bezdomini was dead. Andris' mother said that she recieved only one of the hundreds of letters he had sent to her, but receiving that one letter and knowing her son was still alive gave her new strength. Andris read his mother's letter over and over, at least 100 times. His mother had been ailing when he last saw her, and he considered her living through a second hell in Siberia a miracle. A year after he received the letter from his mother, he received a letter from his sister. She informed Andris that their mother had died in her sleep at the age of eighty-four.

One day while shopping in downtown Hartford, Andris spied a familiar face in the crowd. It was a man he had known in the Ukraine, a Russian policeman whom everyone had feared, for he was a devout communist of brutal character. Andris, shocked to see this man in Hartford, started walking towards him. The Russian recognized Andris before he could reach him and he ran, fleeing through the crowd in panic. Andris chased him, but the man disappeared down a side street.

This strange encounter was not nearly as startling as the one he experienced only a few months later, when a knock came at the front door of his home. He opened the door to see a heavy set elderly man grinning at him through a wrinkled time-worn face. Tears began streaming down the man's face, and he began to shiver but he didn't move. He just stared at Andris, waiting for recognition. Andris started to ask the man what he wanted and why he was crying, but then the face, the sparkling eyes, the wide grin, made his mind race through time. That same man had stood before him many years before at his parents' home in the Ukraine. It was his old friend Nicholas Gatzi, who had been shot in the head by the Russians three times and left for dead on the frozen pond behind Andris' house. Even Gatzi considered it a miracle that he lived. Andris was overjoyed to see his old friend whom he had given up for dead. Gatzi had also become an American citizen and had settled in New England.

I have not seen nor heard from Andris in many years, and I assume he is still living happily in Hartford, Connecticut. I do think of him often, especially when my stomach grumbles. His dark journey and miraculous survival are always fresh in my mind. I have met many remarkable persons in my time, but none quite as remarkable and courageous as this quiet Connecticut Yankee.